Amazing Grace
MAZES & more!

Anita Reith Stohs

Illustrated by Ed Koehler

SAINT LOUIS

To James, Daniel, David, Isabel, and Margaret Safarik.
May God's amazing grace
surround you all your days.
(Ephesians 6:24)

Amazing Grace

You have been saved through the gift of God's amazing grace (see Ephesians 2:5). The gift of God's grace has been given to everyone—moms, dads, brothers, sisters, grandmas, grandpas, and *you*!

Follow the letters of the words AMAZING GRACE to find your way through the maze.

Sing these words to the tune of "Amazing Grace."

Amazing grace,
How great God's love
To save a child like me.
I once was lost, but now I'm found;
From sin I now am free.

God's Great Love

God's love is so great! For Jesus' sake, He fills our lives with His great love—His most amazing grace. Because Jesus took our sins to the cross, God the Father promises to take us to heaven someday (see John 3:16).

Follow the heart shapes through the maze.

We grow in God's love each day.

The Best Book Ever

In God's Word, we read about His amazing grace for us. We read about how God took care of His people—God rescued Jonah and God rescued Daniel. But best of all, we read that Jesus died for us and rose again. Do you know what book is called God's Word?

Look at the top grid below. Copy the lines from the top boxes into the correct boxes at the bottom. (You can find the correct boxes by using the code. Find the letter to the left, then count across to the right number.)

Look in God's Word to find stories of His grace.

What a Wonderful World!

In the beginning, God made the world and everything in it. He was very pleased with what He had made (see Genesis 1:1–31). What do *you* like best in God's world?

Look at the two pictures. Find 10 things that are different.

Thank God for making our wonderful world.

God Creates
the First People

After God finished creating the rest of the world, He created the first people. Who did God make to live in His wonderful world (see Genesis 2:7;22)?

Use a thick crayon to color in the line from start (see arrow) to finish. Do you know the name of the first person God made? Do you know the name of the second person?

God made you too.

Adam and Eve Sin

God gave Adam and Eve one rule to follow in the garden. But Adam and Eve disobeyed God and brought sin into the world (see Genesis 3:1–24). God still loved Adam and Eve though He did not like their sin. He gave them the first promise of a Savior.

Who would that Savior be? Go through the word SAVIOR to see.

God sent Jesus to save the world from sin.

Protected from the Flood

Many years after promising to send the Savior, God kept Noah and his family safe from the biggest flood ever. When the water started to dry up, Noah sent a dove to see if it was dry enough to leave the ark (see Genesis 7:17 and 8:6–12).

Follow the line to find what the dove found.

God keeps you safe.

God's Promise to Abraham

God made a special promise to Abraham. Although Abraham was very old, God promised he would have many children, and grandchildren, and great-grandchildren. One of the descendants of Abraham would be very special (see Genesis 15:1–6).

Who would that special person be? Cross out all of the names that are the same to find out.

Joseph

Isaac

Jacob

Esther

Mary

Isaac

Jesus

Jacob

Mary

David

Esther

Joseph

David

Sing the song "Father Abraham."

Abraham's Faith

God blessed Abraham with many, many children and grandchildren. Jesus also came from Abraham's family—the Savior who saved the whole world from sin. Abraham did not do anything to deserve such a great honor. He was a sinner—just like you and me. But Abraham had faith and God blessed him (see Genesis 15:6).

Follow the pathway through the word FAITH to find Jesus.

Like Abraham, you are saved by faith

Jacob's Dream

Jacob, Abraham's grandson, went on a long trip. One night he dreamed of a stairway to heaven. There were angels going up and down the stairs and God was at the very top. In his dream Jacob heard God promise that He would never leave him (see Genesis 28:10–22).

Follow the pathway through the maze from God to Jacob.

God's Plan for Joseph

Joseph was Jacob's son. His brothers were jealous and sold Joseph as a slave to Egypt. Then he was put into prison. God was with Joseph in prison. God helped him get out of prison so he could save his family and other people (see Genesis 37:12–45:28).

Help Joseph find his way out of prison.

God is with you in times of trouble.

Eating on the Run

God's people became slaves in Egypt, but God promised to rescue them. They ate a special meal the night before God kept His promise and led them out of Egypt (see Exodus 12:1–30).

Follow each line and write the correct letter on each blank. Then you will know the name of this special meal.

God keeps His promises.

The Ten Commandments

After they left Egypt, God gave His people the Ten Commandments (see Exodus 20:1–17). The Ten Commandments show us our sin. They show us our need for a Savior. Jesus came to be that Savior.

Follow the letter "J" to find your way through the maze.

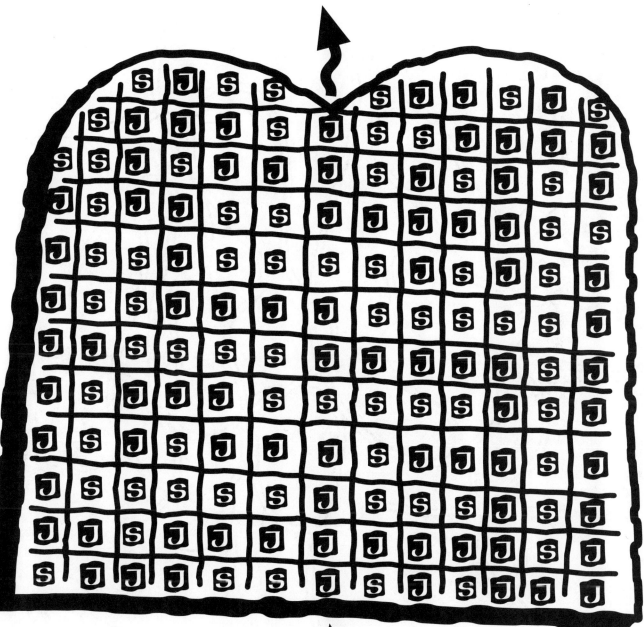

Jesus kept the Ten Commandments in our place.

Israel's New King

God sent Samuel to anoint David—the one He had chosen to be the new king for Israel. David became the King of Israel many years later (see 1 Samuel 16:1–13).

Find the path that takes Samuel to David.

God chose you to be His child.

Mary's Good News

One day an angel told Mary, "You will have a baby. He will be God's Son. You are to give Him the name 'Jesus.'" Mary hurried to tell her cousin Elizabeth the good news (see Luke 1:26–56).

Follow the path Mary took to Elizabeth's house. Read the song of praise Mary sang when she arrived: "My soul glorifies the Lord and my spirit rejoices in God my Savior."

Praise God for sending Jesus to be your Savior.

Born in a Stable

Mary and Joseph went to Bethlehem where Jesus, the Son of God, was born in a stable. His first bed was a manger (see Luke 2:1–7).

Follow the maze through the manger.

Jesus was God's great Christmas gift to the world.

Glory to God!

"Christ the Savior is born," an angel told some shepherds. Suddenly a choir of angels appeared in the sky. "Glory to God in the highest!" they sang (see Luke 2:8–14).

Follow the words of the angels to the shepherds below.

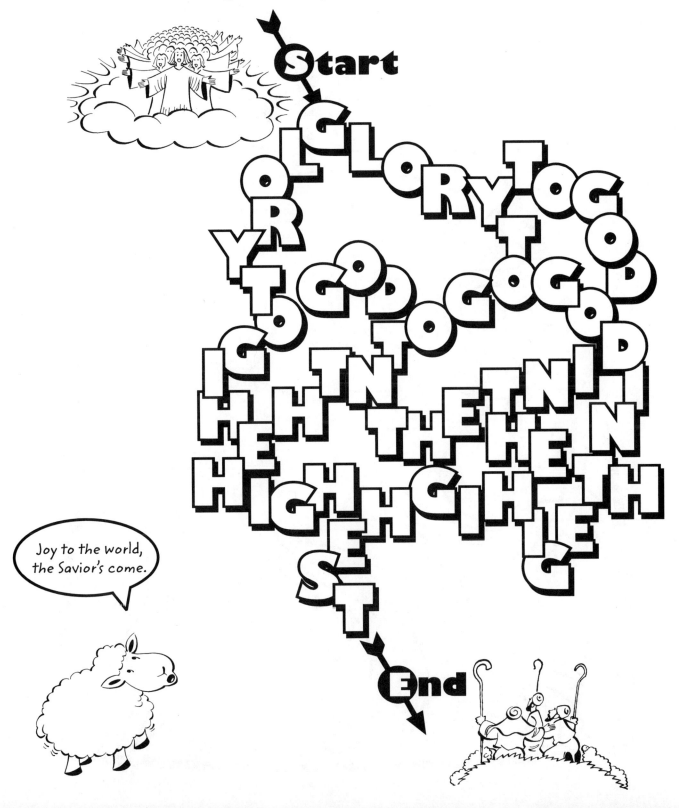

Jesus Is Baptized

When Jesus was baptized, the Holy Spirit came down from heaven as a dove. God the Father spoke from heaven and said that He loved Jesus, His one and only Son (see Mark 1:9–11).

Use a crayon to trace the outline of a dove.

Fishermen Follow Jesus

"Come follow Me," Jesus told some fishermen. And they did! The fishermen became Jesus' disciples (see Mark 1:14–20).

Help the disciples follow Jesus. Find the path that has *only* footprints.

Jesus calls you to follow Him too.

Jesus Feeds 5,000

Jesus told many people about God's love. One day, more than 5,000 people came to hear Him. When it was time to eat, they did not have enough food. Jesus made a little boy's lunch into enough food to feed everyone (see Matthew 14:13–21).

God gives you your food today. Find six things that are different in the two pictures.

Jesus Heals a Little Girl

A little girl was very sick. Her mother asked Jesus to help. Jesus made the little girl well again (see Mark 7:24–30).

Help the mother find her way to Jesus.

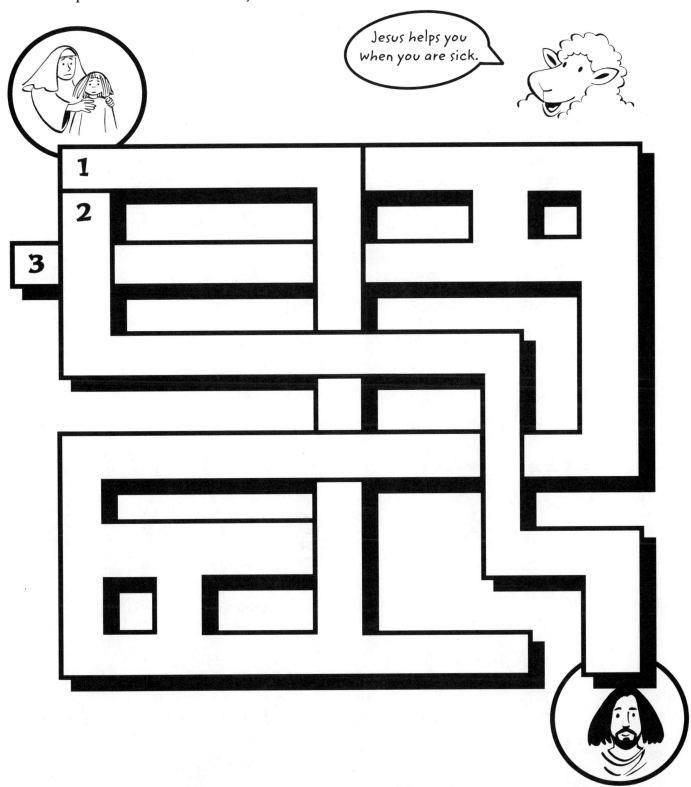

The Forgiving Father

Jesus told a story about a forgiving father who welcomed his long-lost son back home (see Luke 15:11–32). Whatever wrong things we do, God the Father welcomes us back with love. He forgives us and loves us, even when we don't deserve it. That's why God's grace is the best gift we can ever receive.

Help the boy find his way to his father's loving arms.

The Only Way to Heaven

Jesus is the Way, the Truth, and the Life (see John 14:6).

Jesus is the only way to heaven. He is waiting for you. Follow the maze to see if you can find the path to heaven that Jesus has already marked out for you.

The Special Meal

The night before Jesus died, He took some bread and wine and gave it to His disciples. He said the bread was His body and the wine was His blood. Then Jesus told the disciples to eat bread and drink wine in this very special way to remember Him (see Luke 22:7–20).

Jesus grants us forgiveness every time this special meal is celebrated today. Color the letters you see that are on top of the others. Then you will find out what we call this special meal.

God shows grace to His people through this special meal.

Christic Died for Us

Some people did not understand that Jesus Christ was the Son of God. They wanted Him to die and put Him on a cross. Even when Jesus was on the cross, He forgave the people who hurt Him. Then He died for our sins (see Matthew 27:27–50).

Who did Jesus Christ die for? Ask someone to make a copy of this page. Cut out the pieces with words. Put the pieces together to form a cross.

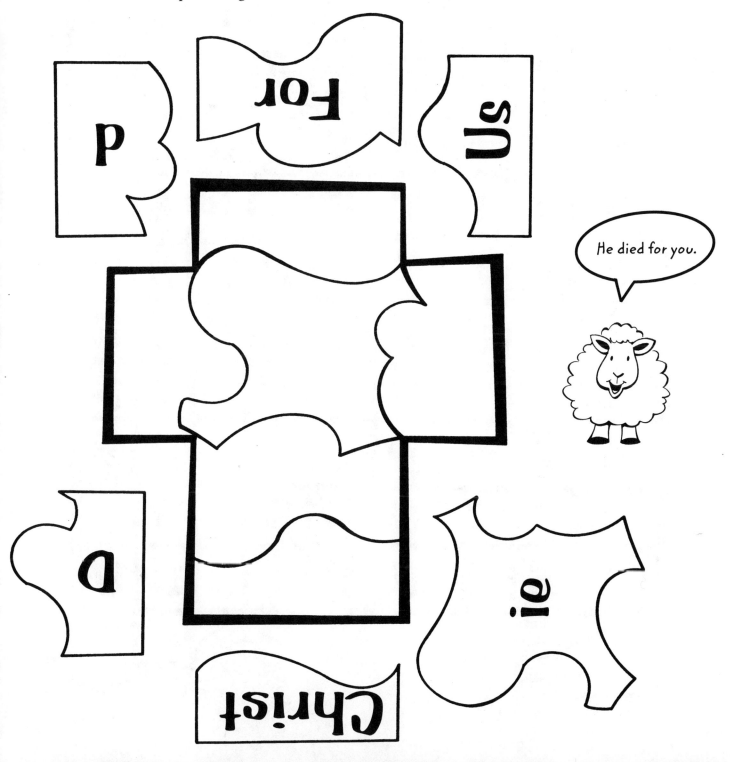

The Good News

Alleluia! Jesus lives!

Early Easter morning some women came to Jesus' tomb. They did not find Him. An angel said, "Jesus is not here; He is risen!" (see Matthew 28:1–7).

Show the women the path to the tomb. Follow the letters in the words the angel said.

E	H	E	R	E	H	E	H	A
O	T	H	E	V	E	I	S	O
L	O	E	R	E	H	N	R	I
S	N	D	T	H	E	R	E	S
I	S	E	O	V	R	E	S	E
S	D	S	N	D	A	H	E	R
U	J	I	L	E	T	H	I	S
S	U	S	D	I	O	A	S	R
E	R	I	N	O	S	I	R	I
J	E	S	U	T	I	S	E	N

The First Pentecost

God sent the Holy Spirit as flames of fire on the first Pentecost Day. The Holy Spirit helped the disciples speak in many different languages. Everyone in the crowd, from all the different countries, was able to hear about Jesus' love in their own language (see Acts 2:1–13).

Find the path through the flame.

God's Love Is for Everyone

"Go to Cornelius," the Holy Spirit told Peter. Peter went to the Roman soldier to tell him about Jesus' love. Cornelius discovered that God's love is for everyone (see Acts 10:1–7).

Help Peter find the best way to Cornelius. Start on the black square, then go to a white square. Go back and forth between black and white squares until you reach Cornelius.

God's love is for all people.

Lydia Believes

Paul told Lydia about Jesus and His love. God opened Lydia's heart to believe in Jesus (see Acts 16:11–15).

Can you find the path to the center of Lydia's heart?

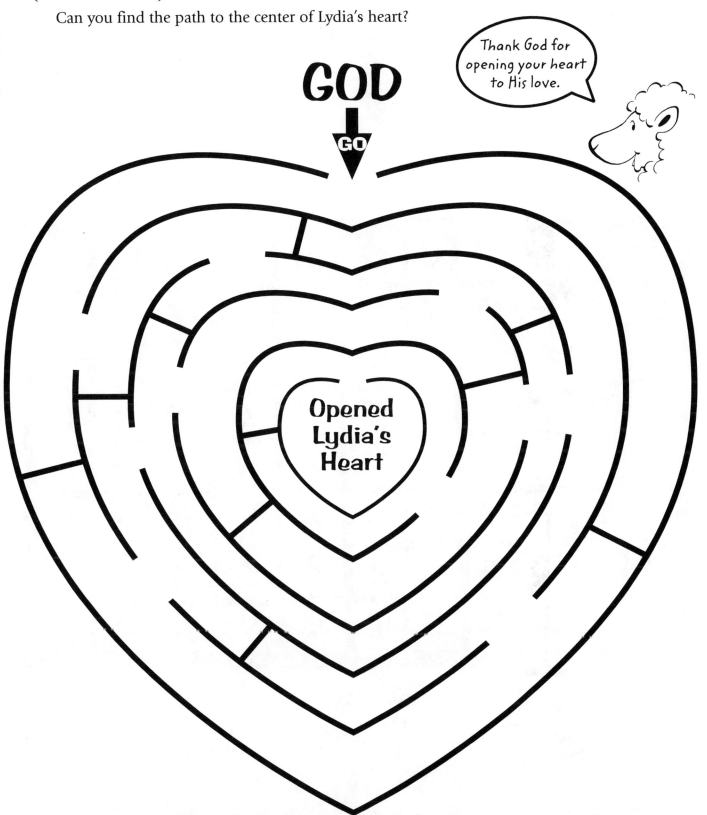

God's Grace Lasts Forever

One follower of Jesus was named John. He wrote the last book of the Bible called Revelation. John ends the book of Revelation with a prayer. He prays that the grace of God will be with all people who believe in Jesus. God's grace will *always* be with us!

Follow the words THE GRACE OF GOD BE WITH YOU to finish the maze.

End

I	T	H	Y	O	U	O	Y	H	T	I
W	E	W	O	Y	O	U	O	B	E	W
D	B	E	W	I	Y	T	Y	I	W	D
O	D	B	D	T	H	T	E	B	E	O
G	O	G	O	H	T	I	W	D	O	G
F	O	F	O	E	C	A	R	A	C	F
O	E	C	G	E	H	E	G	R	E	O
E	C	A	R	H	T	H	E	A	C	F

Start

Sing these words to the tune of "Amazing Grace."

Amazing grace, God's gift to me
Goes with me all my days,
Until in heaven my Lord I'll see
And sing to Him my praise.